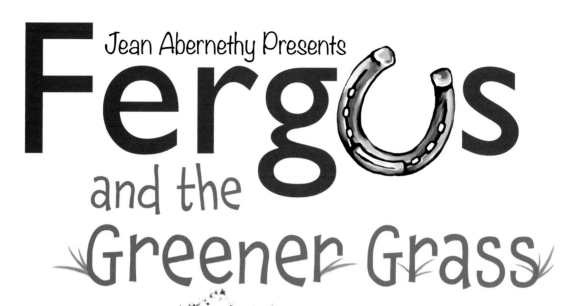

Jean Abernethy Presents

Fergus
and the
Greener Grass

T
TS

TRAFALGAR SQUARE
North Pomfret, Vermont

First published in 2017 by
Trafalgar Square Books
North Pomfret, Vermont 05053

Disclaimer of Liability
The author and publisher shall have neither liability nor responsibility to any person or entity with respect to any loss or damage caused or alleged to be caused directly or indirectly by the information contained in this book. While the book is as accurate as the author can make it, there may be errors, omissions, and inaccuracies.

Trafalgar Square Books encourages the use of approved safety helmets in all equestrian sports and activities.

Library of Congress Cataloging-in-Publication Data

Names: Abernethy, Jean, author, artist.
Title: Fergus and the greener grass / Jean Abernethy.
Description: North Pomfret, Vermont : Trafalgar Square Books, 2017.
Identifiers: LCCN 2017026008 | ISBN 9781570768453 (plc)
Subjects: LCSH: Horses--Comic books, strips, etc. | American wit and humor,
   Pictorial.
Classification: LCC PN6728.F444 A28 2017 | DDC 741.5/973--dc23 LC record
available at https://lccn.loc.gov/2017026008

Book and cover design by RM Didier
Typefaces: Noteworthy, Verdana

Printed in China

10 9 8 7 6 5 4 3 2

For Caroline

Fergus was a little horse,
        outstanding in his meadow.

He was eating grass beside the fence
when came into his head,
Ohhhh...

He had a BIG idea,
    'cause he couldn't quite decide
if the grass might be a little greener
    on the other side.

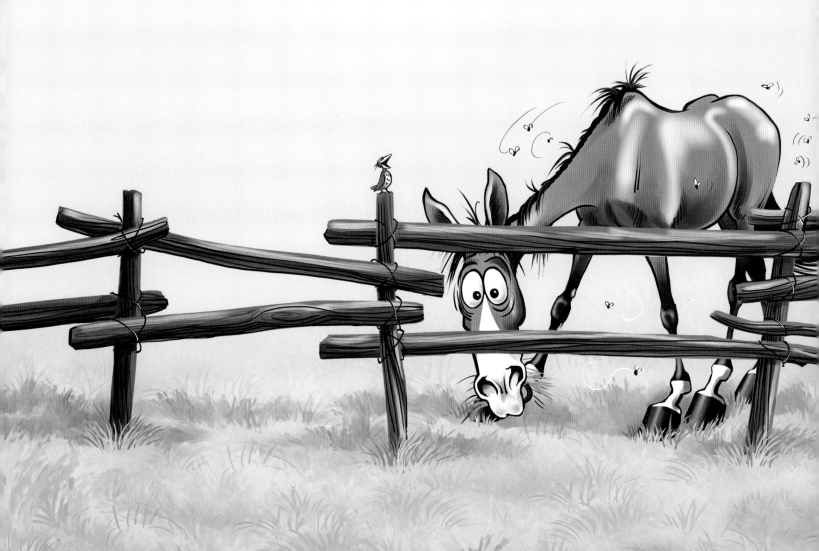

So he reached through,
and chose to chew
the greenest he could see.

That fine spring day, the rails gave way,
and Fergus, then, was **free!**

And so he grazed this pasture
which was greener than the rest,
until he took a longing look
way off toward the West.

Beyond a wooden fence a
greener valley looked exciting!
He stopped to stare
the grass down there
looked tasty and inviting.

He wondered how
he'd reach that grass,
so fragrant, so divine.

But then a horsefly
started chewing
right
on his
behind!

He backed up to address
that itchy spot upon his hide,

and then he landed
horseshoes-up,
on the other side!

When he regained his footing,
his equine dignity,
Fergus was delighted
by the grass that he could see.

He savored every flavor.
Each mouthful was a thrill!

But...

then he spied some greener grass
farther down the hill.

The fence was strong and sturdy,
high and sound and stout and straight.
So Fergus just unhooked the chain...

...and **opened up** the gate.

He dropped his gaze, began to graze
until he reached some wire...

...then saw the grass beyond it,
and raised
his head
up higher.

The grass beyond that wire fence
looked oh-so-very green.
It was the greenest, greenest, greenest
grass he'd ever seen!

The wire was high, and tight and strong,
so he began to wonder,
if he might find a way
to sample it...

...by
reaching
under.

It worked!

Oh my! This grass was tall.
It hid his knees and hocks!

He munched and grazed
until he found
a fence made out of rocks.

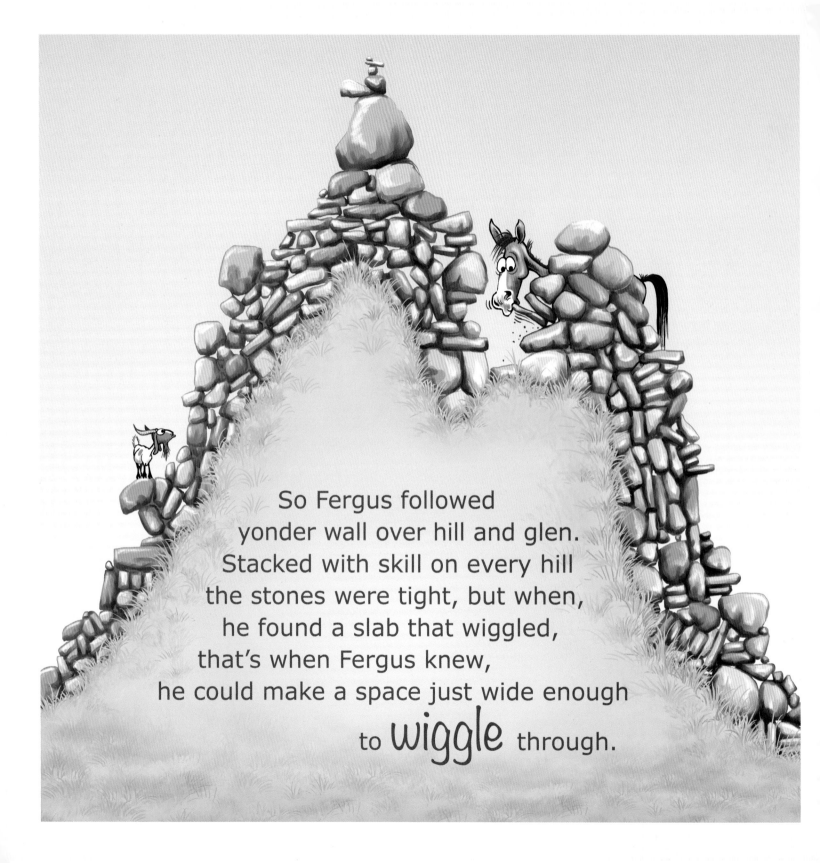

So Fergus followed
yonder wall over hill and glen.
Stacked with skill on every hill
the stones were tight, but when,
he found a slab that wiggled,
that's when Fergus knew,
he could make a space just wide enough
to wiggle through.

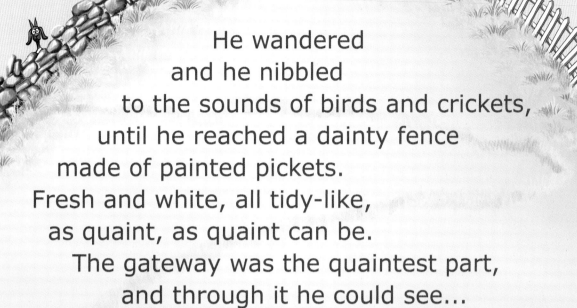

He wandered
and he nibbled
to the sounds of birds and crickets,
until he reached a dainty fence
made of painted pickets.
Fresh and white, all tidy-like,
as quaint, as quaint can be.
The gateway was the quaintest part,
and through it he could see...

...the grass! So smooth, and clipped and green!

Fergus couldn't wait
to take a bite
for sheer delight,
and so
he nudged   the gate...

...oops!

He grabbed a taste, but fled in haste!
This field was full of holes!
He galloped 'til he met a fence
of logs and stumps and poles.

He might have been the firstest horse
to ever learn to climb,
But when he reached the other side
he had the bestest time!

Now Fergus got to thinking
'bout the fences he'd got past,
quite convinced each grassy field
was greener than the last.

So when he reached a wall so high, and oh so very long,
he was absolutely certain there was greener grass beyond.

This one was a **doozey!** But no fence could stop him now.
He had to find a way to...reach the other side...but how?

For miles it stretched
from North to South,
thick, and tall, and wide.

He decided he would jump it,
to reach the other side.

Fergus aimed,
and took a run,

and leapt so high
and grand!

Beyond that fence
there was no grass!

He

had

no

place

to

land.

An itch,
a twitch
upon his shoulders.

Feathers
sprouted there!

They grew to **wings,**
great, graceful things,
that held him in the air!

Fergus didn't fall,
instead he soared up to the sky.
He'd become a **Fergusus** and so began to **fly!**

For miles he sailed
        above the land...

...he circled, swooped, and spun...

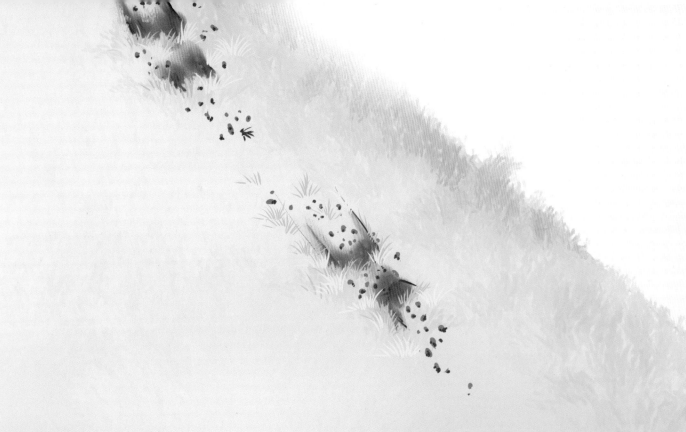

...and finally landed in the meadow,
right where he'd begun!

The great wings vanished in a trice,
and nevermore were seen.
There he sat,
and that was that,
in his meadow green.

Now look at Fergus
standing there,
much older than he was.

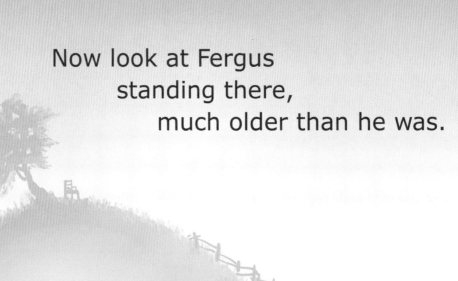

He's wiser now,
and more content
to stay at home, because,

The great wings vanished in a trice,
   and nevermore were seen.
There he sat,
   and that was that,
      in his meadow green.

Now look at Fergus
standing there,
much older than he was.

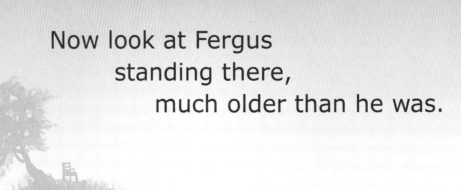

He's wiser now,
and more content
to stay at home, because,

he knows it's not about the grass.
That's just the destination.
He knows it was the fences where
he learned determination.

If life should take him far beyond
the edge of all he's known,
he has faith those wings will grow.
He knows it, 'cause he's

flown!

He's scarred and marred,
from nails and rails,
but wears it all with pride...

...'cause how would he have ever known,
if he hadn't
ever
tried?